P9-DGI-517

SCIENCE
in a Bag

by Sandra Markle

Illustrated by June Otani

SCHOLASTIC INC.
New York Toronto London Auckland Sydney
Mexico City New Delhi Hong Kong

ISBN 0-439-13701-2

24 23 22   8 9/0

Printed in the U.S.A.   40

First Scholastic printing, revised edition, February 2000

Contents

Introduction   4

Grow Your Own Herbs   6

Watch Water Change Color   10

Put Diffusion to Work   13

Create Another Color Change   17

Remove an Egg's Shell Without Cracking It   22

Shrink an Egg   25

Does Yeast Need Sugar to Grow?   28

What Does Yeast Do to Bread Dough?   30

Can a Chemical Reaction Make Dough Rise?   38

Grow a Mold Garden   42

Find Out Why Some Things Float   45

Boat in a Bag   48

Cause a Mysterious Disappearance   50

Save That Fruit   52

Freeze a Treat   55

Trap Some Water   62

Can you remove the shell from an egg
without touching it?
Can you make an egg shrink?
Can you turn bright red water to light
pink as if by magic?
Can you reveal a secret message with
red cabbage juice?
Can you make water disappear?

Yes, you can do all this and more! All
you need are some materials you will find
at home or can buy cheaply at a grocery,
gardening store, hardware store, or five-
and-ten store. Then do the activities in
this book. Find out how science can help
you do some exciting things.

You'll be using large and small self-sealing plastic bags in all of the activities. This will let you safely handle the experiment and get a really close look at what's happening. You may want to have a friend or adult be your partner and hold the bag for you as you set up. For most of the activities, though, you can set the open bag in a sink or metal cake pan. Pour in liquids slowly, and the bag will stay put without spilling. Always double-check that the bag is sealed after the setup. Some plastic bags may also just naturally leak a little at the corners of seams. So with anything that could be messy, place one bag inside another. Or use bags made for freezing because they're made of thicker plastic.

To be a recycling scientist, collect used large and small self-sealing plastic bags, wash them out, and set them in a dish drainer in the sink—upside down with the mouth open—to dry. Also wash and use bags again as you do the activities. That way, you can enjoy investigating and help the earth, too.

Remember

- Do not do any activity using the stove or microwave without an adult partner to help you.
- Clean up the work area after you finish your project.
- Have fun!

Grow Your Own Herbs

Did you ever wonder what goes on underground when seeds start to grow? Now you can sprout some herb seeds and watch the changes take place right before your eyes.

You'll need:

herb seeds
small self-sealing plastic bag

paper towel
paper cup or 6-inch-deep clay pot
potting soil
plate
spray bottle (for misting)

Buy a small envelope of seeds for an herb, such as dill, parsley, basil, or oregano, that your family enjoys using to season food. You can get them at a gardening supply center or five-and-ten store. Wet a paper towel and squeeze out the water. Fold the damp towel into a square that will fit inside a small, self-sealing plastic bag. Spread half the herb seeds on the towel. Be sure the seeds are not on top of each other. Slide the towel into the bag. Seal the bag except for one corner. Lay it flat in a warm spot but out of direct sunlight.

Plant the other half of the seeds. Follow the seed package directions. Use a six-inch-deep clay pot full of loose potting soil, or a paper cup full of soil. If you use a paper cup, poke five small drainage holes in the bottom with a sharp pencil point. Then set it on a plate. Mist with water as needed to keep the soil damp.

Check the pot and bag every day for change. If you have a magnifying glass, use it for a closer look. Every other day, poke a finger inside the bag. If the towel feels dry, open the bag and mist with water from a spray bottle. Check the soil in the pot and keep it moist, too.

As the seeds begin to sprout, the hard seed coat that protected the seed will split

open. Inside, the seed—even if it's a tiny one—has a bit of stored food and an embryo or baby plant just waiting to grow.

Watching the seeds sprout in the bag will let you see what's going on underground in the pot. Which part of the baby plant do you see poke out of the seed first—the thin white root or the stem with the first green leaves?

Continue to let the young plants grow inside the bag. Watch the changes for a few days. During this time, the stored food gives the young plants the energy they need to grow. To transfer the plants to the pot, gently scrape them off the paper towel with a fingernail and press them onto the soil. Continue to watch the plants change as they grow.

When the plants look like the picture on the seed package, harvest a little at a time. Rinse the plants you're going to eat in clean water and add them to foods that call for this herb.

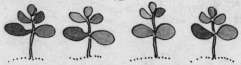

Watch Water
Change Color

You don't need magic to see water change from clear to bright red. You can use science to do it.

You'll need:

2 cups of ice water
2 cups of hot water
small self-sealing plastic bag
bottle of red food coloring
clock with a second hand

Pour two cups of ice water into the plastic bag. Next, drop in three drops of

red food coloring, zip the bag shut, and lift it to eye level holding it at the top. Try not to jiggle it or swish the water around. Check the time and then watch what happens to the coloring.

Streamers of red will sink down from the drops, spreading out in curling waves. Does the red color appear to spread out quickly or slowly? Time how long it takes the water to turn all red.

Everything is made up of tiny building blocks called *molecules*. There are many different kinds of molecules. When there are two different kinds of molecules together, they tend to mix. They spread from where there is more of one kind to where there is less of that kind. This process is called *diffusion*. You can see the red food coloring spreading out and mixing with the water. The currents are made by the moving water molecules.

Now find out what heat does to moving molecules. Rinse out the bag, then pour two cups of hot tap water into it. Drop in three drops of red food coloring and seal. Lift the bag to eye level to watch the action. Check the time as you did before.

What do the spreading currents of color look like this time? How long does it take for the coloring to diffuse through the water? What do you think heat does to the movement of water molecules?

Put Diffusion to Work

You can use diffusion to make a tasty drink.

You'll need:

large self-sealing plastic bag
warm water
3 tea bags

Fill a clean, large, self-sealing plastic bag two-thirds full of warm tap water, then drop in three tea bags. Carefully squeeze out the air above the water and seal. Place the bag flat on its side in a warm, sunny spot. Let it sit several hours or until the water turns a golden brown. Pour some over ice and enjoy (with or without sugar). People often use this method to make tea in the summertime.

From what you discovered before, why do you think the sun helps diffusion brew the tea?

You can also use diffusion to make your room smell good with a scent bag.

You'll need:

small self-sealing plastic bag
1 tablespoon whole cloves
5 bay laurel leaves
dried orange peel (leave peel out over-
    night, or microwave 1 minute)
cinnamon stick

coffee filter
2 teaspoons peppermint extract
pin

In a small self-sealing plastic bag, combine a tablespoon of whole cloves, five bay laurel leaves, pieces of dried orange peel, and a stick of cinnamon. Next, cut one coffee filter into thin strips. Add these to the bag and sprinkle everything with two teaspoons of peppermint extract. Seal the bag and shake gently to mix. After an hour, use a sharp pin to carefully poke many tiny holes in the bag.

Now put the bag in your room. The next time you come into your room, take a deep

sniff. The pleasant odor you smell will be the aroma from your scent bag. It has gradually diffused through your whole room. Such room "odorizers" are called potpourri (pronounced poe-puh-ree). For how many days do you notice the smell? How far from your room does the scent spread?

Create Another Color Change

Certain types of matter are part of two groups called acids and bases. Acids and bases are different. For example, foods containing acids often taste sour. Those containing bases often taste bitter. Some acids and bases are poisonous. Some can damage body tissues, so tasting isn't a good way to tell which things are acids and bases. Here is a useful way to discover acids and bases.

You'll need:

2 cups red cabbage leaves, chopped
saucepan
small self-sealing plastic bag
1 tablespoon white vinegar
household ammonia
lemon juice
baking soda (1 teaspoon dissolved in 4 tablespoons of water)
powdered laundry detergent (1 teaspoon dissolved in 4 tablespoons of water)
apple juice
cotton-tipped swabs
measuring spoons

An *indicator* is a special substance. It turns a different color when combined with an acid. It doesn't turn color with a base. Red cabbage juice makes a good indicator. It contains *anthocyanin*, which reacts with acids and bases. To collect red cabbage juice, chop about two cups of red cabbage leaves. Put them into a saucepan, and add enough water to just cover the leaves.

With an adult working with you, cook on medium heat, stirring until the water looks very dark reddish-purple. Let the juice completely cool. Throw away the used-up leaves. Then test each of the solutions listed in the chart on the next page. Make a copy of the chart and check the boxes to record your results.

To test, pour four tablespoons of the solution into a small self-sealing plastic bag. Add two tablespoons of the red cabbage juice, and shake. Check the indicator box to see what the color shows. Rinse the bag very well with water between tests.

Test Solutions	Slightly Acidic	Very Acidic	Slightly Basic	Very Basic
Vinegar				
White or clear household ammonia				
Lemon juice				
Baking soda (1 teaspoon dissolved in 4 tablespoons of water)				
Powdered laundry detergent (1 teaspoon dissolved in 4 tablespoons of water)				
Apple juice				

Indicator Color Change

Test Solution	Red Cabbage Juice Appears
Acid	Red to violet
Base	Blue-green to green
Neither Acid nor Base	Color unchanged

You may not know it, but acids and bases are everywhere around you—in nature, in industry, even inside you. A kind of acid in your stomach called *hydrochloric acid* helps break down the food you eat during digestion. *Propanic acid* is used to keep foods such as bread from spoiling too quickly. A very strong acid, *sulfuric acid,* is used in car batteries, and to manufacture paints, plastics, and fertilizers.

Bases dissolve fats and oil, so many of them are used to make cleaners. Bases are also used to make deodorants and leather, in antacids and laxatives, and in the manufacturing of plaster.

Now use what you discovered to write a secret message that will appear as if by magic. Pour three tablespoons of water into a small self-sealing plastic bag. Add one-half teaspoon of baking soda, and shake until the powder is well mixed. Use this liquid to write a short message on a sheet of white paper with a cotton-tipped swab. When the paper is dry, brush off any powder left. Send this to a friend with instructions for cooking up some red cabbage indicator and these instructions: "To read the secret message, soak a paper towel in the cabbage juice and press on the paper."

Remove an Egg's Shell Without Cracking It

This sounds tricky, but you can do it with a little science.

You have already discovered that vinegar contains an acid. Although it's a fairly weak acid, it's strong enough to dissolve *calcium carbonate*—the main material in an egg's hard shell.

You'll need:

small self-sealing plastic bag
1 uncooked egg
16-fluid ounce bottle of white vinegar
1 glass

Place the egg in the bag and add enough vinegar to completely cover the egg, or enough to fill the bag about half full. Hold the bag and look closely at the egg's shell. The bubbles you see on it are carbon dioxide gas, just like the bubbles in a soft drink. This gas is given off as the vinegar reacts with the shell. Turn the bag so that the egg is in one corner, and slip this part of the bag into a glass. This will keep the egg underneath the vinegar even when you aren't holding on to the bag.

Let the egg sit overnight. Then lift the bag out of the glass and gently squeeze the egg. Surprise! It will feel soft. Most

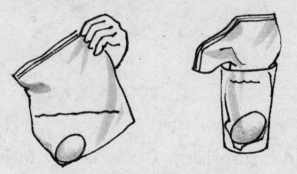

of the hard material in the shell has dissolved and become mixed with the vinegar.

Let the egg sit in the vinegar two more days to let the vinegar completely dissolve the hard shell material. Working over the sink, pour off the vinegar and slip the egg into your hand. Under a trickle of water, very gently rub your fingers around and around on the egg to get off any remaining bits of shell material. When it's all gone, the egg will look like a little water-filled balloon, and you'll be able to see the yolk that's inside.

Did it surprise you that the egg was still whole? The vinegar did not remove the membrane that was just inside the shell. How does the shelled egg feel? When you're finished examining it, slip the egg into a clean, small, self-sealing plastic bag and get ready for the next activity. Then rinse out the bag that contained the vinegar and let it dry so it's ready to use later.

Shrink an Egg

When you did "Watch Water Change Color," you discovered that substances diffuse. The molecules move from an area where there is more of one kind to where there is less of that kind. But there is a change when the diffusing material passes through a membrane like the one around the egg. Substances still tend to move from where there's a lot to where there's very little. But the membrane will only let certain materials pass through it.

A membrane is actually like a screen. The molecules that make up the membrane have space between them like spaces in a screen. The *size* of the spaces between the molecules do not let everything pass through them. Diffusion through a membrane is called *osmosis*.

Water will always pass through a membrane. Here's how you can prove this.

You'll need:

1 small self-sealing plastic bag
clear corn syrup
shell-less egg
1 glass

Fill a small self-sealing plastic bag about half full of clear corn syrup and carefully slip the shell-less egg into it. Don't be surprised that the egg floats. Take a close look at the size of the egg. Set the bag in a glass as you did before to keep the egg in the corn syrup.

After a couple of hours, check the egg. Does it look bigger or smaller than it did? Leave the egg overnight before checking again. How does the size look now?

Leave the egg in the syrup solution for three days. You should be able to tell that the egg has shrunk by now. This happened because the water inside the egg moved through the membrane into the syrup. But the corn syrup did not pass through, en-

tering the egg. Working at a sink, open the bag and remove the egg, gently rinsing it under running water. The membrane will now appear to be a loose sack, and you'll be able to feel the yolk that's inside the egg.

Can water move the other way through this membrane? To find out, slip the shriveled egg into a bag half full of water and let it sit supported by the glass overnight. Were you surprised to see the egg swollen once again?

Now use what you've discovered about osmosis to tackle this challenge. The celery sticks you cut for a snack are limp. To help make them firmer, should you soak the sticks in plain water or salt water? After you've made your prediction, test your idea.

Does Yeast Need Sugar to Grow?

Yeast is a type of plant. Green plants are able to make their own food as a type of sugar. Yeast isn't green, though, so is it still able to make its own food? You can easily set up an experiment to find out.

You'll need:

2 small self-sealing plastic bags
2 packets dried yeast—the kind used
  in baking
1 teaspoon granulated sugar
1/2 cup lukewarm water
permanent marking pen

Each yeast plant is a tiny oval. As it grows, it produces one or more small bumps that soon break free and become new yeast plants. In the process, the plants give off alcohol and carbon dioxide gas. If the yeast is growing, you'll be able to smell an odor made by the alcohol. And you will see a froth made by the carbon dioxide gas.

If yeast makes its own food, just adding water will be enough for it to grow. If it *doesn't* make its own food, only the yeast given a food supply of sugar will grow. Here's a way to find out!

Pour the contents of one packet of yeast into each of the bags. Mark one bag with the pen, and add the sugar to it. Next, pour half of the water into each bag and seal it, carefully squeezing out the air. Holding on to both bags, shake gently for about a minute.

Check the bags every fifteen minutes. Which is growing—the yeast with sugar, or the yeast without sugar?

What Does Yeast Do to Bread Dough?

In the experiment you just did, you found that yeast plants won't grow unless they have a food supply. Most bread recipes call for adding yeast, but why? To find out, follow the steps below to make some bread.

You'll need:

2 large self-sealing plastic bags
1 packet dried yeast
1 teaspoon sugar
2 teaspoons vegetable oil

1 cup warm water
2 1/2 cups flour
1 egg
strip of masking tape
fork
measuring cup (1 cup)
measuring spoons
cookie sheet
1/8 teaspoon cooking oil
3 paper towels
pot holders
oven

Set the bags side by side in the sink with the open ends up. Break the egg into the cup. Beat it with a fork until the yellow and white are mixed together well. Pour half of the egg into each bag. Next, rinse out the cup, fill it with warm water,

and pour half of the water into each bag. Add 1/2 teaspoon of sugar to each bag. Add the yeast to one bag, marking it with the tape. Seal and shake both bags gently to mix.

Return the bags to the sink, reopening the tops. Add 3/4 cup flour and one teaspoon oil to each bag. Seal the bags again and squeeze gently to mix well, about one minute for each bag. Open the bags, add another 3/4 cup flour, and seal. Start squeezing the bags until all of the flour is blended into the dough. Add 1/4 cup more flour and squeeze again. Seal the bags and wait thirty minutes.

Wash and dry your hands. Open the bags and examine the dough balls. In what ways do the two dough balls look different? Feel different?

Now, press the air out of each bag and zip shut. Place the bags side by side in a warm shady place for an hour.

Preheat the oven to 425 degrees Fahrenheit.

Pour 1/8 teaspoon oil onto the cookie sheet and spread evenly with the paper towel. To turn the dough balls out, open the bags over the greased cookie sheet and slowly turn inside out, pushing the dough until it is free. Keep track of which dough contains the yeast. Bake for ten minutes or until golden brown on top.

Remove from the oven with an oven mitt and let the bread completely cool, then break off a piece of each loaf. In what ways does the bread containing yeast look like the bread prepared without it? In what ways is it different? Now eat a piece of each loaf of bread. What differences do you notice in flavor and texture?

You no doubt noticed that the bread made with yeast was much lighter and softer than the loaf made without yeast. Why is that? You already discovered that when yeast plants have food and grow they give off a gas. Because wheat flour is naturally elastic, the rising carbon dioxide bubbles stretch the dough. Baking the bread causes the gas to leave the dough. But not before the dough surrounding the gas bubbles has hardened. Look closely at the bread and you'll see the holes left by the gas bubbles. Finally, the heat kills the yeast plants so they don't continue to grow in the baked bread.

No one knows who first used yeast to make bread rise. But it's generally believed to have happened in ancient Egypt. Loaves of raised bread were found in the

tombs of the pharaohs. In one idea, it was a happy accident. Yeast floats in the air like dust. Someone probably saw that a wheat dough left open to the air began to rise. People began saving a little bit of a rising bread dough as a starter for the next batch.

Today, breads are made from many different grains. There are also different types of wheat bread, such as white and whole wheat. The next time you go to the supermarket, count how many different types of bread are available. Ask your parent to buy several kinds of bread, such as rye, pita, whole wheat, and croissants for you to compare. Which has the smoothest texture? Which tastes the sweetest? Which is the most elastic? Think of at least two other ways you could compare your bread samples.

Fast Facts About Bread

- Wheat flour is made from wheat berries. They grow clustered at the tip of a stalk. Before the wheat berries can be ground into flour, they have to be separated from the hard husks or chaff.

- To grow, yeast needs to be moist, have sugar for food, and be about 100–110 degrees Fahrenheit—a little warmer than the human body.

- In ancient Egypt, bread was such an important food that it was sometimes used as money. Today, the word "bread" is sometimes used to mean money.

- In the Middle Ages, you had to be a noble or a priest to be allowed to eat white bread. That's because it took a lot of time and effort to remove all the bran or outer coatings from the wheat berries. The bran coating made the bread brown. Removing the bran really makes bread less healthful.

- In the Middle Ages, bread was not only an important part of a meal, it was the plate, too. Food was often put on slabs of unraised bread called trenchers. They soaked up meat juices. After the meal, the trenchers were given to the servants, the poor, or the dogs.

- Early settlers and traders who traveled across North America often carried flour and a bit of dough starter with them so they could make bread anywhere they went. Because the dough starter had a sour smell, these people were sometimes called "sourdoughs," and so is the bread.

Can a Chemical Reaction Make Dough Rise?

The bread you just made rose because the yeast grew, giving off gas. What if you didn't have any yeast, though? Could a chemical action do it? Try this experiment to find out.

You'll need:

1/2 cup flour
2 small self-sealing plastic bags
water
cooking oil
paper towel
1/2 teaspoon baking powder
marking pen
2 greased pie plates
pot holders
oven

Wet one spot on the paper towel with cooking oil and wipe the inside of each bag. Also wipe the pie plates.

Preheat the oven to 400 degrees Fahrenheit.

Next, pour half of the flour into each bag. Add the baking powder to one bag and mark it with an X. Seal and shake gently to mix. Add two teaspoons of water to each bag, seal, and squeeze to mix. Remove the two lumps of dough and place on the pie plates. Keep track of which plate contains the baking powder.

Bake for eight minutes or until at least one appears golden brown. Remove and let completely cool.

As you can see, the baking powder made the dough rise. Like yeast, baking powder gives off carbon dioxide gas, and water is enough to start the reaction. Check the kind of container the baking powder came in. You'll understand now why it's made to help keep this powder dry.

Now, follow the recipe below to use this chemical reaction to bake biscuits.

Grandma's Favorite Biscuits

2 cups flour
1 tablespoon baking powder
1/3 cup margarine
1 cup milk
1 large self-sealing plastic bag
tablespoon
cooking oil
pie plates, or cookie sheet
pot holders
paper towel
oven

Grease the inside of the bag and the pie plates or cookie sheet as you did before and preheat the oven to 450 degrees Fahrenheit.

Put the flour and baking powder into the bag, seal, and shake.

Let the margarine sit out until it's soft, and then add it to the bag.

Seal and squeeze the bag to mix.

Finally, add the milk, seal, and squeeze to mix again.

Spoon by the tablespoon onto the pie plates or cookie sheet. Bake at 450 degrees for ten to twelve minutes, or until golden brown on top. Makes about sixteen biscuits.

Remove finished biscuits from the oven and cool until just warm before eating them. How does the taste of the biscuit compare to that of the yeast bread? How does the texture compare?

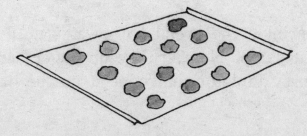

Grow a Mold Garden

Just like yeast, molds are a type of plant called fungi. Unlike most plants, though, fungi don't have true roots, stems, or leaves. And they don't have chlorophyll. Chlorophyll is a green coloring material that, with sunlight, helps a plant to make its own food. So to grow a mold garden, you need food as well as water and a warm place to grow. Since they don't make their own food, these plants don't need sunlight.

You'll need:

1 slice of bread (stale bread is best)
1 large self-sealing plastic bag
1 tablespoon water
magnifying glass

Sprinkle the bread with water until it's quite damp. Next, rub your finger across a dusty tabletop and wipe it on the damp bread. Slip the bread into the bag and seal it.

Place the bag inside a dark, warm spot, such as a cupboard. Wait three days and then check. If the bread looks dry, and you don't see any fuzzy-looking spots, open the bag and sprinkle on more water. Then reseal and wait another three days.

After a while, you'll see fuzzy white patches with blue-green or brown spots. That's mold. Examine it through the bag. Take an even closer look with the magnifying glass.

Mold grows from spores rather than seeds. These are so tiny that they float in the air with dust. That's why collecting some dust to spread on the bread was a way to "plant" your mold garden. When the spores begin to grow, they grow into a large mess of thin white threads. They spread out in all directions. These threads push into the food material. Then they give off a substance to break the food down. They take in this food to help them continue to grow. Eventually, the mold develops special "fruiting bodies" that make spores. These are the dark spots. Take a close look through the magnifying glass.

Continue to look at your mold garden every few days. Measure the size of the main mold growth daily. How quickly is it spreading? How does the bread change as the mold grows?

Molds have been called nature's recyclers. In nature, molds wouldn't use up all the food they grow on. What's left would be put back into the soil to help green plants grow.

Find Out Why Some Things Float

You already know that some things float while others sink. But why? You can find out by performing this test.

You'll need:

large self-sealing plastic bag
permanent marking pen
paper
pencil
Styrofoam packaging peanut
penny
dried soup bean
wooden building block
ball of modeling clay
pebble
ice cube

First, use a permanent marking pen to draw a line straight across one side of a large plastic bag (about halfway up). Hold the bag under the tap until the water level

is at the colored line. Next, make a copy
of the chart below. Then rest the bottom
of the bag on the counter, holding the sides
up with one hand. Set the first item on
the test list on the water's surface. Check
the column that shows if the object floats
or sinks. If it floats, carefully lift the bag
with both hands and observe how much of
the object is below the waterline—one-
fourth, one-third, one-half, or more. Write
down this amount in the Water Level column. Test each item this same way. Be
sure to save the water test bag for the
next investigation.

Test Results

Object	Water Level	Floats	Sinks
Styrofoam packaging peanut			
penny			
dried soup bean			
wooden building block			
ball of modeling clay that measures no more than two inches			
pebble			
ice cube			

Now you know that objects that float don't just ride on top of the water. An object sinks until it displaces or pushes away an amount of water equal to its weight. Water is denser or thicker than air. When the weight of the object pushes away its own weight, the water holds up the object and it floats. What if an object goes down and down and is underwater, or on the bottom, before it pushes away enough water to be lifted up? It sinks!

If your test bag was deeper, do you think some of the items that sank might float? The next time you're soaking in the tub, take along the test objects and check out your idea.

Boat in a Bag

Now that you know what makes something float, try this: Shape the ball of modeling clay you used in the earlier test into a shape that will float.

First, plan and then build your clay boat. To test it, rest the bottom of the bag on the counter, holding up one side of the top, while you set the boat on the water's surface. If the boat floats, lift the bag with both hands to eye level and check how much is underwater. If the boat doesn't float, try a different shape.

Once you've made a boat that will float, try this. Can you build a boat that will hold at least twenty dried soup beans? Try it, loading your boat before setting it afloat.

If it sinks, quickly scoop out the beans. Find a way to shape the boat differently so that it will float. If it floats, try adding more beans, five at a time, and test again. How many beans can your boat hold before it sinks? Could you make a boat that could hold even more weight and stay afloat?

You probably discovered that the more bowl-shaped you made your boat, the more weight it could carry. A bowl shape makes an empty space below the waterline. The space pushes away or displaces water and the weight of the clay. So the space helps to lift up the weight.

Shipbuilders say that how deeply a ship "rides" in the water is its draft. Ships have lines called *plimsoll* lines painted on their side to show how deep a ship's draft should safely be when it's loaded. A ship riding very low in the water moves more slowly. It is more likely to take on water and sink if caught in a storm with high waves.

Cause a Mysterious Disappearance

You can make bright red water turn light pink easily once you know the science of bleach.

You'll need:

small self-sealing plastic bag
water
bottle of red food coloring
eyedropper
liquid chlorine bleach
tablespoon

Fill the bag half full of water. Add three drops of red food coloring. Add one tablespoon of bleach, seal the bag, and shake gently. The color should look lighter. Add-

ing more bleach, one tablespoon at a time, should make the coloring become so light that it disappears or can hardly be seen.

The coloring disappears because when chlorine mixes with water, it pulls oxygen atoms out of the water. (Water is made of hydrogen and oxygen atoms.) These oxygen atoms then combine with the red dye atoms. This makes a new compound or combination of atoms. This new compound has different properties—one is that it's colorless.

The same thing happens when bleach is used on clothes. It makes stains seem to fade. It can also make colored clothes fade, so it's important to use bleach with care.

Save That Fruit

Have you ever had a banana or an apple you were eating turn brown before you finished it? You may be surprised to learn that oxygen in the air made this color change happen.

You'll need:

small self-sealing plastic bag
apple sliced in half
paper towel
lemon or orange juice

To see this for yourself, slice an apple in half. Place one half inside a small, self-sealing plastic bag, squeeze out most of the air, and seal. Set the other half on a paper towel so that the cut side is open to the air. Check every thirty minutes for two hours. The half open to the air will start to turn brown first and will get much darker.

The fruit turns brown because the oxygen in the air reacts with the fruit's cells. It breaks them down in a process like digestion. It was impossible to remove *all* the oxygen from inside the bag. But the bag protected the fruit from being open to more than a little oxygen.

Vitamin C can be used for even more protection against the oxygen in the air. To prove this, slice away the outer side of both apple halves so they're both light-colored once again. Dip one in lemon or orange juice; these both have vitamin C.

Then set both apple halves side by side, open to the air. You will see that the half with the juice coating stays light.

Now, use what you learned to make a fruit salad you can carry with you. Cut bite-sized chunks of apples, bananas, and orange slices and put them in a small, self-sealing plastic bag. Squeeze the juice from one orange slice over all the fruit. Press the air out of the bag and seal it. When it's time for lunch or a snack, this fruit salad will still look fresh and taste great.

Freeze a Treat

How can salt help you turn yogurt into a frozen snack? Just follow the steps below to find out.

You'll need:

2 small self-sealing plastic bags
1 large self-sealing plastic bag
4.4 ounces (snack size) flavored, blended yogurt
spoon
8 cups crushed or small ice cubes
2 cups rock salt
old towel
plastic garbage bag
scissors
bowl

Spoon the yogurt into the smaller bag. Gently press to

let out air, and seal. Slip this bag inside the second small bag and seal. Fill the large bag about one-fourth full of crushed ice or ice cubes. Sprinkle on  rock salt. Place the bag of yogurt in the center of the ice. Continue adding ice, then salt, then ice again until the small bag has ice all around it. Seal the big bag.

Wrap the bag in the towel, spread out the garbage bag, and begin to gently roll the bag over and over on the garbage bag. From time to time, look at the yogurt bag inside the towel to see if the yogurt is firmly frozen yet. Also, make sure the

large bag is tightly sealed. The yogurt will take about fifteen to twenty minutes to freeze.

Open the big bag and take out the small bag. Close up the large bag and throw it away. Rinse off the outside of the small bag. Open and enjoy!

How does the ice melt and the yogurt freeze? The rock salt causes the ice to melt. Heat energy is needed for this melting process. The ice draws heat from the air and, more importantly, from the yogurt.

A Frozen Treat's Ice-Cold History

It's hard to imagine a time before frozen yogurt and ice cream. In ancient times, though, it was hard to chill things unless you lived where it got cold enough to make ice or snow naturally. Rich Romans used to send slaves to haul snow down from a high mountaintop. The snow was mixed with fruit juice, honey, or wine. The first ice cream—of sorts—was made by the ancient Chinese. They added milk to their flavored ices. Marco Polo, the noted traveler, helped spread this recipe.

No one is quite sure who first experimented and discovered that milk or cream would freeze by covering it with ice rather than mixing the two together. But it seemed to happen about the time Europeans began using sugar and chocolate. At first, the nobles of England and France tried to keep the recipe for ice cream a secret. But it finally got out. Restaurants

in France began to serve ice cream to people in the late 1600s. The recipe then spread with the settlers that came to North America.

In those days, ice cream was made in pewter bowls. The one with the cream and flavoring was placed inside the one with the ice. Then the whole thing was jiggled and shaken while the ice-cream mixture was stirred. This was necessary to make the finished ice cream smooth. Then someone found that adding salt to the ice made the ice cream freeze faster. Later, the

hand-cranked ice-cream freezer was developed. It made the job easier. Still later, machines powered by electricity made making ice cream a snap.

Ice-cream lovers didn't stop experimenting, though. They came up with ice-cream sodas, sundaes, Eskimo Pies, and ice cream on a stick. When an ice-cream vendor at the 1904 World's Fair in St. Louis ran out of paper dishes, he served his ice cream in a thin waffle rolled into a cone. Presto—the ice-cream cone was invented. Ice cream has also been made in an amazing number of flavors. But vanilla is still the favorite.

Fast Facts About Yogurt

- People have been enjoying the tangy taste of yogurt in Iran, Turkey, and other Middle Eastern countries for thousands of years. In the United States people have been eating it more and more since the late 1970s.

- Yogurt is made from the milk of cows, goats, sheep, camels, and water buffalos. Most yogurt eaten in the U.S. is made from cow's milk. Like milk, yogurt can be healthy for you. It has calcium, protein, and phosphorus in it.

- To make yogurt, harmless bacteria is added to milk and kept warm. The bacteria changes milk sugar into lactic acid. This makes the fluid milk thicken. That gives yogurt its custard-like texture.

Trap Some Water

A special chemical called *polyacrylamide* can absorb water and hold onto it. But how much water can this chemical trap?

You'll need:

small package of Water Grabber crystals (available at florists, or at stores carrying gardening supplies)
small self-sealing plastic bag
measuring spoons

Pour just one-half teaspoon of the Water Grabber crystals into the bag. Add one teaspoon of water, seal the bag, and massage gently to mix. You'll see that the crystals soak up all the water. They swell into gelatin-like beads. Next, repeat the process. This time add more water one teaspoon at a time. Massage until you no longer see any water around the beads at the bottom of the bag. Then tip the bag to see if any water drains out.

How many teaspoons of water can you add before the Water Grabber cannot trap any more water?

Water Grabber is added to the soil so plants can be watered and left for a long time. You already know that molecules are what makes up things. The molecules of polyacrylamide are hooked together into long chains. They coil in a way that makes lots of natural folds. Through osmosis, which you learned about in "Shrink an Egg," water goes into the chain of molecules and fills up the spaces in the folds. Just as a sponge soaks up water, more and more water is absorbed by the polyacrylamide molecules until all the spaces are full. Water tends to move from where there is a lot of it to where there is less. So as the soil around this chemical dries out, the action is the opposite. Water is let out into the soil. A water-trapping chemical like this is used in super water-absorbent diapers.